POSITIVE TRAINING FOR REACTIVE DOGS

TABLE OF CONTENTS

Before you start reading, scan this QR Code to get all bonus content!

CHAPTER 1: UNDERSTANDING REACTIVE AND AGGRESSIVE BEHAVIORS IN DOGS

Reactivity can be hard for dogs; without support, your dog can become hostile.

You want to take your dog for a relaxing walk, but they start barking frantically at the sight of another dog or a human, prompting you to haul them away. This is a reactive dog, meaning it overreacts to everyday events that other dogs would ignore. Although reactive dogs aren't always violent, aggressiveness can develop from reactivity, so paying close attention to training becomes important.

Common triggers excessively stimulate reactive dogs. It may be difficult to manage them and get them out of the situation because they may lunge, bark, or growl as they fixate on whatever is causing the reaction. A nervous dog will frequently become reactive. Genetic factors can play a role, but lack of socialization, unpleasant experiences in the past, or inadequate training are more probable causes.

Aggressive dogs see similar symptoms but are motivated to injure and wreck property. Any reactive dog might be provoked into hostility; therefore, treating them seriously is important.

Beware of aggressive dogs.

In an ideal world, you wouldn't want a reactive dog. Adult dogs can be observed or taken for a "test run" walk, but forecasting a puppy's behavior as an adult can be more difficult.

Since puppies frequently adopt their parents' characteristics and reactivity can have a hereditary component, Dr. Katherine Houpt, the James Law Professor Emeritus of Behavior Medicine in the Department of Clinical Sciences, recommends meeting the parents of a litter if possible. Visit the litter before weaning if that isn't possible. Although mother dogs should not be violent, they protect their puppies. Puppies should approach you for attention rather than retreating or hiding and should be pleasant, self-assured, and extroverted.

Finding the triggers

Finding the precise triggers that upset your dog is the first step. According to Houpt, a trigger is anything that serves as a stimulus to cause your dog to respond violently. This might be a strange person, other dogs, or both. Typical scenarios include a person with a crazy hat, bearded guys, pets, and kids.

While some dogs might react to these stimuli in all circumstances, others might only react in certain circumstances. When not on a leash, some dogs get along with other dogs just fine, but leash reactivity sets in when they are. Other dogs could be more inclined to respond aggressively in confined or crowded areas or when out for a nighttime stroll.

Once you've discovered your triggers, try to avoid them when developing a training program. You don't want the action to develop into a habit. Houpt advises avoiding the dog park and walking your dog when no one else is there.

Safeguard your dog

Putting your dog in uncomfortable settings can make them more fearful and might worsen their behavior. Be cautious when walking your dog outside. If you see a person or dog likely to upset your dog, avoid them if possible. Allow your dog to go on some relaxing walks and other activities so you can compliment them on their good behavior, and they can start to unwind.

Remember that not every person or dog has to get along with your dog. According to Houpt, the belief that all dogs should adore all other people and dogs is mostly an American phenomenon.

She claims that although dogs can roam freely in Italy, they are kept apart from other dogs, and people don't always approach them to pet them. By respecting a dog's personal space, they treat their dogs more like people in this way.

You must speak out for your dog. For instance, shield them from an approaching stranger to prevent them from needing to defend themselves. Tell the individual politely but firmly that your dog is doing well, timid, or in training if they keep approaching them or try to pat them. After hearing this, Most people will typically understand the need to respect your space.

Counterconditioning

Of course, avoiding something won't work forever. The long-term solution is to teach your dog coping mechanisms so that their triggers become less frightening through behavior modification and counterconditioning.

Start by carrying snacks with you at all times. "Reward the dog as soon as the trigger appears," says Houpt. Give them snacks as you walk by or when the frightening thing passes. At first, you will want to give the reward at a safe distance from the trigger, if possible, so your dog feels comfortable. It could include, for instance, keeping a soccer field's worth of distance between you and a group of young players.

Your dog will begin to identify the trigger with something nice with continuous training. Hopefully, they will spot another dog eventually and come to you for a reward. Positive reinforcement techniques can also utilize rewards and toys.

You will eventually be able to get closer to the frightening stimuli. To ensure that you are in charge of the issue, enlist the aid of a buddy. If your dog, for instance, responds to other dogs, invite a friend with a calm dog to cross the street from where you and your dog are working, all the while using rewards to redirect and encourage your dog's concentration. Ask your friend to get a bit closer if your dog continues to be calm and attentive to you. Ask your buddy to move further away if your dog becomes anxious. You can do this, for instance, with kids or adults wearing caps.

Make a strategy for working with your dog over time to help him link triggers with a pleasant treat (or toy or praise), making them less frightening. If you are having problems, see a fear-free dog trainer or a veterinary behaviorist to develop customized training methods for your dog.

DOG REACTIVITY VS. DOG AGGRESSION

Aggression is not reactivity; nonetheless, it can intensify.

One of the most frequent causes for pet owners to seek expert assistance for their dogs is aggression. What, though, is aggression? Aggression is any aggressive, harmful, or destructive conduct directed against a person or an animal, whether human or another species.

To effectively address the situation, it is crucial to identify the source of hostility. Dogs can grow aggressive because of fear, frustration, prey drive, pain, or the need to protect their territory, resources, or family members. These circumstances can push a dog too far, causing it to swiftly change from reactive, afraid, or guarding behaviors to violent ones.

Acts That Can Occasionally Lead to Aggression

Reactivity: Aggression and reactivity are sometimes mistaken. Reactive dogs overreact to specific stimuli or circumstances. Reactivity can be brought on by genetics, a lack of socialization, self-control training, an upsetting experience, or a combination of these factors, with fear frequently acting as the catalyst.

Reactive dogs have specific triggers, such as when the dog feels restrained on a leash, individuals wearing hats or beards, or young children. The greatest thing you can do is give a reactive dog room if he approaches you. Do not try to meet him by approaching. Working with a trainer to try behavior modification methods that will address the source will help avoid the escalation of aggressiveness if you have a reactive dog.

Fight or Flight: The most frequent catalyst for hostility is fear. Normally, a dog would prefer to flee from whatever is troubling him when he is terrified or feels threatened. When a dog is surrounded or confined and unable to escape, he may engage in combat to defend himself. Only their body language may serve as a warning when a dog is fearful. Bites are often fast snaps that might happen when the victim walks away and turns his back.

If people were aware a dog can see their conduct, even when we believe it to be friendly, as dangerous, there would be fewer bites. For instance, a dog can feel frightened if we bend down and reach to pet the top of his head. Lack of socializing is another major factor in canine phobias. A dog is less likely to be scared if it has favorable early encounters with many people, sounds, and environments. It will also be helpful to teach a dog to unwind when handled.

Resource Protection - Dogs are known for protecting objects they perceive to be of high value. Toys, food, bones, sleeping quarters, and even humans can be among these goods. This propensity arises because dogs are derived from wild predecessors that had to guard their resources to live.

This habit can be reduced by teaching dogs commands like "leave it," "out," and "place" or "off." Another effective strategy for dealing with resource guarding is to trade with your dog, offering him the item he is guarding in exchange for a reward or to step away from the dog's bowl while it is being fed and dropping a treat inside.

Leash Reactivity - Leash-reactive dogs tend to snarl, bark, and/or lunge in the direction of objects that frighten or frighten them. These triggers can be particular, such as children, males, people wearing hats, or male/female dogs, and they can be other dogs or humans. Dogs who exhibit these actions attempt to avoid a fight by removing the threat or putting more space between themselves and it.

Acts That Have the Appearance of Aggression

The following are a few of the actions that are frequently mistaken for aggression:

Puppies mouthing or nipping one another interact with the world through their mouths. Puppies can get mouthy and nip more forcefully than necessary when they play with other dogs or their owners. An angry puppy does not do this nibbling but rather one who is overstimulated and in need of a rest.

Rough Play - Play amongst dogs is a common occurrence in dog interactions. Dog play is pretend combat. Puppies pick up the proper technique from their classmates. However, as long as both dogs are having a good time and respecting each other's body language, dog play can be a terrific activity for socializing and exercise. Dog play can become intense, noisy, and look violent.

Physical Pain - A dog that starts snarling or snapping may be ill or in discomfort. Dr. Jerry Klein, the AKC chief veterinary officer, advises owners to take their dogs to the vet for an examination to rule out a medical reason if the behavior is unusual and manifests suddenly.

Bodily Expression

Dogs use their body language to communicate with other canines and people about various circumstances because they cannot speak. Everyone should be aware of some typical dog body language cues.

Signs of a friendly dog include:

Relaxed body

Happy expression, soft mouth

Tail wagging

Play bow

Relaxing ear

A relaxed tail wag or a body-wide wiggle

Crouching with the belly up

Leaning in for a pet

Compassionate glance, frequent blinks, and soft eyes

SYMPTOMS OF ANXIOUSNESS

Not being weary but yawning

Licked lips

Unexpected scratching

Sniffing

Panting

Body with tail tucked under

SYMPTOMS OF AROUSAL

Ears pointed forward, mouth shut

Strong eyes with more white showing

Body tight and forward

Wags its tail high and gently.

Raised fists

Signs that precede a bite:

SIGNS OF AROUSAL OR ANXIETY

Dedicated eye contact

displaying the eye whites

Growling

Displaying teeth

Uneasy body

Seeking expert assistance if you think your dog is violent is essential. You can get a recommendation for a licensed animal behaviorist in your region from your veterinarian. The Association of Professional Dog Trainers, the Certification Council for Professional Dog Trainers, and the International Association of Animal Behavior Consultants are further resources. You must be careful not to expose your dog to circumstances that might trigger aggressive behavior.

CHAPTER 2: THE POWER OF POSITIVE TRAINING

Positive training is not a scientific term.

Although it is a happy event, welcoming a new furry friend into your life comes with obligations, and training is one of the most crucial. Dog training is more than simply teaching skills; it's also about developing a close relationship with your dog, ensuring they're secure, and encouraging peaceful cohabitation. In this chapter, we'll examine dog training in general and show how positive reinforcement can make your dog a well-behaved, obedient pet.

Why Train Your Dog?

Dog training is more than just teaching your dog instructions; it's an investment in their wellbeing and your bond. Effective training improves communication so you can comprehend your dog's wants and requirements. A trained dog is also safer since it will obey orders that can stop mishaps and keep them safe. A well-behaved dog is also a joy to have around, improving both you and your quality of life.

The Influence of Positive Reward

The days of severe training techniques based on fear and punishment are long gone. Effective, compassionate training relies on positive reinforcement. This technique rewards desired actions with sweets, compliments, or play. Your dog is more inclined to repeat positive activities associated with those outcomes. This method fosters confidence and trust between you and your dog.

Start with the fundamentals.

Start your training off with simple instructions like "sit," "stay," "come," and "heel." Focus on one command at a time, and keep training sessions entertaining and brief. When your dog does well, thank them with cookies or a beloved toy and show them how much you appreciate them. Keep in mind that during this procedure, patience is your best friend.

Maintaining Consistency

Dogs thrive on stability and routine. Encourage family members to use the same verbal and nonverbal cues as you do and to use the same hand gestures. Consistency aids in your dog's comprehension of expectations and hastens the learning process.

Socialization

The socialization of your dog is a crucial step in their training process. To help them become more confident and avoid behavioral issues, expose them to various people, animals, places, and situations. Their capacity to adapt increases and anxiety in novel settings decreases through proper socializing.

Identifying and Solving Challenges

You could run with obstacles like stubbornness or diversions during exercising. Be patient and, if necessary, modify your training methods. If you're having trouble, think about hiring a professional dog trainer. Their knowledge can provide perception and answers suited to your dog's particular characteristics and requirements.

Creating a Bond for Life

Training isn't only about teaching orders; it's also about creating a relationship that will last a lifetime. Engage in things you both like while spending quality time with your dog. Play, walks, and cuddles help you feel closer to each other and reinforce the good habits you've been working on.

The Positive Training Four Pillars include:

The application of constructive criticism

Avoiding using physical force, terror, or intimidation

A comprehension of the often misunderstood concept of dominance

A dedication to comprehending dog experience from the dog's perspective

These four components work together to form the
Positive philosophy of positive training. Without each of these, the philosophy is incomplete and less potent and successful in creating enduring bonds of trust and respect between you and your dogs.

The Positive Training Four Pillars include:

1. The application of constructive criticism.
2. Refraining from using coercion, violence, or terror.
3. An understanding of the sometimes misinterpreted idea of dominance.
4. A dedication to taking the dog's perspective to comprehend the dog's experience.

Pillar 1 - positive reinforcement

The behavioral science community has unanimously recommended using positive reinforcement techniques as the most efficient, enduring, kind, and secure approach to training dogs.

Positive reinforcement, in essence, states a higher likelihood of a behavior being repeated if it is rewarded. These techniques are a cornerstone of the core of positive training when combined with negative punishment (the temporary removal or withholding of something the dog wants, such as food, attention, toys, or human contact) or the use of a vocal interrupter to redirect undesirable behavior onto desired behavior and to help a dog make the right decisions. Positive training is frequently criticized by conventional, old-school trainers who claim that it demonstrates ineffectiveness and a lack of leadership, but the fact is that the most admired and effective leaders can bring about change without resorting to coercion.

Pillar #2 - Avoidance of Punitive Methods

According to scientific research, teaching dogs with aggressive, harsh methods doesn't work over the long haul but exacerbates the aggressive reaction and makes already violent dogs even more hostile. Although it is a very straightforward notion, it can sometimes be challenging for dog owners to remember that putting out fires with fire typically leads to someone getting burnt.

Modern behavioral science has thus spoken out against the use of compulsion training, but for the majority of us, our instincts already tell us that rewarding conduct is preferable to punishing it. Many who support traditional training contend that the electric shock or quick kick to the dog's ribs they administer as punishment is not harmful. There are several levels of punishment, and everyone must eventually decide how far they are prepared to go for themselves. But if they can help it, most normal people would want to avoid doing anything that might cause their dog to suffer pain or fear, no matter how little that punishment might be.

Pillar #3 - Understanding Dominance

The largest obstacle to our ability to have genuinely healthy, useful relationships with our dogs is our common misunderstanding of dominance and how it functions inside the dog world. Anyone who has heard a trainer mention how they must be the "alpha," "top dog," or "leader of the pack" to keep things in check and ensure that the owner and their dog have the right kind of chemistry has seen firsthand how pervasive this incredibly misguided belief has become in our contemporary culture.

It's true that during the previous 50 years, scientific knowledge of this idea has evolved and has remained fairly sophisticated. However, in its most basic form, the best approach to explain the problem of dominance as it pertains to our pet dogs is to reassure you that it is not as important as you probably think it is. Dogs do not necessarily fit into the popularly believed hierarchy positions that humans so frequently assign them, nor are they on a road to conquer the world if left uncontrolled.

The most crucial thing for the average dog owner to comprehend is that their dog's disobedience results from them seldom trying to impose control over their person.

Positive training is most effective when the root cause of a dog's misbehavior is correctly identified. However, misdiagnosing the root cause of a dog's misbehavior as dominance typically sets off a chain of events that results in unbalanced, unconfident, and ultimately unhappy dogs (and owners).

Pillar #4 - Using the dog's point of view

You cannot develop a close relationship with your dog without properly understanding how your dog sees the world. However, you must first learn his language and respect his sensory perception to accomplish this.

Even though we are only beginning to comprehend the dog's sense capabilities, it's logical that they play a crucial role in the dog's experience since the senses are strongly tied to emotions, which drive behavior. Dogs can acquire knowledge and resolve any behavioral difficulties they might be experiencing through a technique known as sensory education, which involves using their senses.

Meanwhile, our responsibility as the more evolved species is to learn how to "talk dog" rather than expecting dogs to pick up English (or any other language). By doing this, you will lay the groundwork for a stronger bond and will be more equipped to deal with any challenging behaviors your dog might exhibit.

We must provide the dogs with the self-assurance and resources they need to live and survive in our odd, human world because we have tamed dogs for thousands of years.

Various names, including reward-based, force-free, and positive reinforcement, refer to positive training methods. All of these interconnected ideologies' proponents agree that educating animals using the general idea that rewarding positive behavior increases its likelihood of repetition is far safer, more efficient, and more compassionate. Similarly, it is more probable that instances of behavior will diminish if you ignore or divert it. These ideas and the knowledge that dogs are not wolves attempting to rule us to gain "top dog" status make up the foundation of positive training.

Dogs do not need to be controlled using dominance-based punitive methods.

Dog training is a time and energy commitment that yields a lifetime of love and happiness. Your dog can learn, develop, and thrive with the help of positive reinforcement training in a loving setting. You're laying the groundwork for a well-behaved, joyful, and self-assured furry family member by emphasizing positive interactions and constant direction. So be ready to embark on a thrilling voyage that will turn your dog into a well-mannered, adoring friend!

POSITIVE REINFORCEMENT FOR YOUR DOG

Training your dog will be one of the main tasks you face as a new dog owner.

After conducting a short internet information search, most new dog owners will find themselves overwhelmed by various opinions on the best dog training method.

Positive reinforcement is a common theme throughout both concepts, whether you identify more with the force-free training idea or prefer the techniques utilized by balancing trainers.

Finding the correct incentive is key to teaching your dog effectively.

Let's talk about the advantages of using positive reinforcement with your dog so you can get off to the proper "paw" in your training.

In addition, I'll explain why this is a crucial component of any training plan and how to implement this strategy into your daily training schedule.

Positive Reinforcement Training: What Is It?

All types of dog training can be divided into four groups based on how they induce a dog to alter its behavior. These groups consist of:

Giving your dog a treat for sitting is an example of positive reinforcement, which involves rewarding your dog or adding something to the situation.

Negative reinforcement is when something is taken away to promote a desired behavior (for example, applying pressure to the leash to encourage your dog to lie down and then releasing it after they have finished).

When your dog exhibits an undesirable behavior, you can discipline them by pulling back on the lead (if they move out of a heel without being let go). This is known as positive punishment.

Negative Punishment: Depriving your dog of what they enjoy if they exhibit undesirable behavior (for example, if they play rough and you stop, standing motionless to dull the pleasure of their preferred game).

Dog owners can decide which methods best reflect their ideals by knowing the differences between these groups.

For instance, positive and negative reinforcement can be useful, although it is generally agreed that positive reinforcement is the most effective. Why?

The foundation of positive reinforcement training is the notion that your dog genuinely wants to follow your instructions.

Using training goodies as a positive reward is the most popular method. However, you can apply this method to almost anything your dog considers important.

This involves playing with their favorite game or toy and giving them your praise and undivided attention.

What Justifies the Use of Positive Reinforcement?

As I've indicated, many experts agree that positive reinforcement is the most potent and successful training method.

This helps develop a dog's enjoyment of the training process and encourages your dog to acquire the desired behavior and retain the training lessons.

A dog that enjoys training will be more attentive throughout your training sessions. Your chances of success will be enhanced as a result for many years.

How to Include Positive Rewarding in Your Dog's Training

Finding your dog's motivation is the first stage in any positive reinforcement dog training program. Some dogs only want food, while others don't care about training rewards.

Pay attention to what your dog finds exciting.

Are they prepared to say or do anything to get you to engage in a game of tug?

Do they light up when you compliment them or focus only onthem?

Give them their preferred incentive every time your dog exhibits the required behavior during training.

If you were teaching your puppy to sit, you would give them the treat as soon as their hindquarters touched the ground.

They are more likely to sit the next time you ask them if they understand that doing so results in a treat (or other incentive).

When you are certain your puppy has mastered the behavior, you can gradually reduce the incentive by giving it every second or third time.

Don't, however, completely exclude incentives from the equation. Continue rewarding them on occasion to strengthen your future training.

6 Advantages of Positive Rewarding Your Dog

1. Raise a Puppy with More Confidence

Instead of focusing on punishment-based training, provide an atmosphere where your puppy can grow and develop without worrying about doing it badly.

As a result, they feel safe and secure, which gives them the confidence they need to feel at ease in unfamiliar settings.

This is a terrific approach to bolster your puppy's confidence and assist them in overcoming their concerns if they are afraid or worried.

Although it will take some time, seeing your timid puppy progress is very satisfying.

2. Develop a passion for exercise

You are probably concentrating on teaching the basics of obedience in the early stages of your training adventure. But training doesn't have to finish after your dog has learned these abilities.

At any age, training is an excellent method to engage with your dog and stretch their cognitive abilities.

Positive reinforcement has several advantages, including that your puppy will grow to like training sessions.

They anticipate working with you because they relate training to good, joyful things.

3. Involve the entire family.

This aspect is frequently neglected because dog trainers, particularly those who practice positive reinforcement, are often adults.

Families with kids frequently wish to involve them in caring for the family dog. This includes giving the dog food, engaging in play, and participating in the training procedure.

A little youngster won't have the strength or maturity to realize when it's proper to use pressure to persuade your puppy to sit.

However, most kids get the concept of rewarding their dogs for good behavior.

Allowing your kids to participate with you throughout training and handling praise and rewards is a good idea.

This kind of involvement will delight many kids just as much as their pets!

4. Promotes Intellectual Enrichment

Positive reinforcement for dogs is an excellent technique to stimulate your puppy's brain.

This eliminates boredom, supports proper brain function, and helps to exhaust even the most spirited dog.

Your puppy has to consider what you are asking of them and how to get their treat when you give them a command.

This is among the causes for why many vets advise including obedience training in your dog's daily routine at all stages of their life.

5. Preventing Possible Behavioral Problems in the Future

When investigating issues like dog training, it's crucial to remember that society is always changing and developing.

This implies that the greatest advise now may change from that in the past ten or twenty years.

There was a period when the immediate effectiveness of unpleasant instruments and training techniques was extensively endorsed.

However, recent research has shown that harsh training techniques might harm your dog's health and happiness in later years.

Later in life, dogs who have been educated in this manner exhibit higher tension, anxiety, and stress.

This is particularly crucial when dealing with dogs that may be genetically predisposed to aggressiveness or reactivity or those who have had traumatic experiences in the past.

6. Enhance Your Connection

The bond you share with your dog is powerful. For many dogs, the relationship alone is sufficient motivation to exhibit desirable behaviors.

They care about you and want you to be content. They wish to get your admiration.

When you base your training on positive reinforcement, you'll keep fortifying this connection throughout training sessions.

It enables you to lay a strong foundation of respect and trust that will benefit you and your dog as time passes.

You are not alone if this is your first exposure to the advantages of positive reinforcement training.

There isn't enough conversation on this subject among new dog owners.

With this knowledge, you can pick the most effective training strategy for you and your dog.

Remember that you are not required to employ any particular one of the four training categories.

Additionally, you'll need to incorporate dependable routines, rules, boundaries, and expectations into your chosen training strategy.

There is no denying that training is a significant commitment and takes time and persistence.

However, dedicating this time to your puppy early in your relationship will prepare you for a long, fulfilling life together.

DEBUNKING COMMON MYTHS ABOUT DOG AGGRESSION

An aggressive dog is potentially deadly; thus, managing them calls for specialized help and training. However, dog aggressiveness is considerably more complex than most pet owners realize. One of dogs' most prevalent behavioral issues is a misunderstood subject due to popular beliefs.

Eradicating Common Myths About Dog Aggression

A good dog never snaps at people.

It's impractical to anticipate your dog never displaying hostility, no matter what happens. It would be like asking someone to never disagree with anyone.

Dogs typically show aggressiveness to explain their position to others when fearful, furious, nervous, or disappointed. It is a typical method of dog communication. They may snarl, snap, lunge, or bark furiously in such situations. Even well-mannered dogs that do well in obedience school occasionally exhibit these symptoms.

Aggressive dogs are hostile from birth.

Even while some dogs are genetically predisposed to being forceful, this rarely results in aggression. It is incorrect to attribute a dog's undesirable behavior to its nature. As a defense strategy to protect themselves from prospective hazards, they often learn it from prior experiences.

Violence happens without warning.

Dogs often use non-aggressive behaviors to express their pain or discomfort, such as yawning, avoiding direct eye contact, and licking their lips. Things can worsen if you can't read and comprehend their behavior. You might not have seen the aggressive behaviors if you believe your dog suddenly attacked. Pay attention to your dog's body language to spot the warning signs. Additionally, by doing this, you'll be better able to identify the trigger and catch their emotions in the future.

Dog aggression is universal.

In general, dog owners view all aggressive dogs as threatening or endangering other people or animals. Dog hostility comes in a variety of forms, including the following:

Fear of violence

aggressive pain

Aggression triggered by frustration

Territorial hostility

Aggressive defense

Although each form of dog aggressiveness may begin with warning signs like growling, stiffness of the posture, or snapping, you should handle it differently. To understand the type of hostility people display, it might be helpful to consider the cause of their negative behavior. Doing this lets you comprehend what they aim to gain from such circumstances and take appropriate action.

A hostile dog always acts inappropriately.

Many people believe that a dog is no longer safe to be around if it exhibits any symptoms of aggressiveness. Knowing that a dog's aggressive behavior does not necessarily sum up its character is helpful. To recognize the context and grasp the source of the aggressiveness, you must act appropriately. They'll probably act properly after the trigger has been removed.

The primary motivation for aggression is dominance.

It's a common misperception that dogs attempt to dominate people, so they get hostile towards them. However, aggression against others is typically brought on by fear or worry. It occurs due to their attempts to protect themselves from an intimidating object.

A dog that has bitten someone cannot be controlled.

Pet owners frequently believe that if a dog attacks a person or animal, you can never trust them again. However, they can benefit from expert dog training that includes sensible strategies and astute management. If your dog has bitten someone, it is vital to get an accurate assessment from the professionals because experiences differ.

Only large dogs experience issues with aggressive behavior.

Contrary to common assumption, even tiny and large dogs can be hostile. Due to the possibility that their bites would not be as harmful as those of larger dogs, many dog owners find it amusing when little dogs behave tough. Knowing that they frequently overact aggressively to compensate for their small stature is helpful. In this situation, it is sensible to solve the issue with knowledgeable dog trainers for aggressive dogs. They can offer advice on how to handle your dog's aggressive behavior.

Aggressive dogs should be disciplined for their bad behavior.

Many people believe that punishing aggressive dogs would reduce their behavior. They frequently use severe methods like shock collars or abrasive leash punishments to discipline them. However, investigations and research indicate that these approaches are unsuccessful and can worsen the situation. Dogs do not learn what humans want by being punished for their actions, which may make them more anxious and frustrated. Because of this, professionals who teach aggressive dogs employ careful management and positive reinforcement to control aggressive behavior.

Aggression-Prone Dogs Only Need Obedience Training

Many dog owners believe an obedience course is the best way to deal with aggressive dogs. However, even well-trained dogs can be hostile since they may still misbehave despite knowing how to sit, stay, heel, or lie down when asked to. This is so that it can vary according to the source of assault. It does not imply, however, that you should not teach your dog to heed your directions. One benefit of obedience training is that it makes it easier for you to have a loving relationship with your dog.

COMMON REACTIVITY MYTHS

Reactivity Myths

Reactivity myths appear to be encouraged by owners' needs to explain or identify the causes of their dog's problems. It's quite acceptable to seek explanations; these myths represent many people's ideas of what those explanations might entail. It's simple to accept incorrect things when you don't know much about dog behavior or reactivity, especially when they appear convincing.

Naturally, as reactivity increases in popularity today, reactivity myths also increase in frequency. So, let's put on our Mythbuster hats and debunk as many myths as possible about reactivity.

Myth 1: Previous Abuse

This is so prevalent, especially with pets whose background is unknown, like those from rescues. Many dog owners wish to use this form of justification to explain away a dog's cowering, tense reactions, barking, and other behaviors. In my experience, around half of the rescue dog owners I speak to note that they believe their dog has a history of abuse, even though I am aware that the subset of owners I encounter is biased toward dogs and owners coping with difficulties.

I want to be clear that these owners do not believe that the dogs suffered from a singularly horrific event but rather from systematic and repetitive mistreatment.

If this misconception about reactivity were accurate, dog cruelty would always be prevalent and violent in our culture. Animal abusers certainly occur, without a doubt, but not in the quantities necessary to account for every reactive dog. 50% of all dogs rehomed or saved is a truly astounding percentage.

Myth 2: You Need More Interactions!

This is one of the most seriously risky reactivity myths out there. More interactions with the things that your reactive dog struggles with are not necessary. This puts the dog in an unfair and stressful situation and makes the reactivity turn into biting. Additionally, this is frequently done erratically, such as taking an aggressive dog to a park. That situation begs for a battle.

Consider it from a more human standpoint. The best way to overcome a person's phobia of spiders is not to make their daily activities more filled with them. This does not affect treating the person or lessening their fear. Instead, they need to be on higher alert and experience much less serenity.

Reactive dogs that are forced to interact with their triggers or overexposed to them in the hopes that they would learn to cope with them experience this. To the dismay of their well-intentioned owners, so many of the dogs I work with have histories as dog parks and doggy daycare pets. It's a typical catalyst for reactivity and ought to be avoided!

Myth #3: There is no discipline

Many dog owners are interested in learning the causes of their dog's reactivity and have many questions about them. For some, there is also the concern of what if I have done something wrong. Was I overly cordial? Did I mistreat my dog? Was I supposed to be firmer? Was I not a good teacher of discipline?

No, is the answer.

Reactivity is a dog's emotional reaction. Correcting or penalizing the dog for having them won't help change these overreactions. These things won't help the dog cope with their triggers, teach them coping mechanisms, or help them realize their trigger isn't harmful. Instead, the reverse occurs.

The dog discovers that negative events occur whenever the trigger is present. The punishment also casts a darker shadow over the worry, fear, irritation, or other feelings that a specific dog is now experiencing. It's a disaster and won't make things better.

Reactivity has a variety of causes and influences, all specific to dogs and their way of life. I can guarantee it wasn't because you were overly forgiving, delayed discipline, or showed your dog too much joy and affection.

Myth #4: The Instinct to Protect

No, while they are experiencing a reactive episode, your dog is not attempting to defend you.

Dogs try their best to act in every situation to their best advantage. A dog will react if they believe doing so would improve their situation. They are mostly concerned with themselves.

Truly, the pedestal that people place pets on is peculiar. There are strange myths about loyalty, a "good" dog's tolerance level, and the sixth sense for bad guys. These beliefs about dogs and their function in society distort reality and have serious repercussions, such as the startlingly high rate of dog attacks on children.

This doesn't suggest that dogs have never shown protective behavior, but it depends much on the breed and the circumstances and doesn't seem like reactivity.

Myth #5: Receiving rewards would worsen the situation

Emotions are what drive reactivity. A feeling cannot be rewarded in any way. Rewarding a dog won't make them experience more fear, anxiety, irritation, or other bad emotions, but we can give them a feeling more good or negative. The emotions and reactions are happening to the dog; it's not anything they choose to do.

Consider it this way. Does discovering a lottery win during a depressive episode guarantee that the individual will experience greater depression in the future? Both in people and dogs, emotions don't function in this way.

Rewarding the dog helps us change how they see their triggers. By employing incentives, we can finally reduce the importance of something frightening and make it no longer frightening. It's the most effective technique to modify any behavior in a dog since we can do all kinds of things with incentives to change how the dog views the trigger.

Bonus myth: The man who first proposed the "Dog Is Trying to Be the Alpha" Dominance idea has refuted it. There is no such thing as a dog acting aggressively in an attempt to advance in an imaginary social structure inside an imaginary pack. Simply said, it is a total farce. For wolves or dogs, no aspect of the dominance paradigm holds! This mentality must be abandoned for the sake of all pets and owners since it is terribly outdated.

Dogs do not wish to argue with humans. Even if their actions go against what we would want, they are not acting this way to be obnoxious, to be the alpha or leader, or to show any other form of disdain for their owner. That is not how canine behavior functions and is not the motivation behind any activity a dog takes.

Simply said, your dog is not attempting to engage in any behavior that would put them in opposition to you.

The Truth

As stated in a few of these reactivity myths, the dog's emotions are mostly to blame for reactivity. This frequently triggers a behavioral reaction, such as barking, lunging, snarling, etc. These two elements combine to produce the chaotic behavior of a reactive dog when exposed to its triggers.

Although some of the contributing components may be the same, the underlying reasons for these emotions come from various sources and are unique to each dog. In the end, the reactive dog has trouble dealing with their triggers. The overreaction is the dog's attempt to try and make things better since they can't manage them.

Our reactive pets require assistance and care the most. The most effective way to learn how to accomplish it is through an experienced trainer.

CHAPTER 3: LAYING THE FOUNDATIONS: BASIC TRAINING PRINCIPLES

8 Basic Commands To Teach Your Dog

Southerners pride themselves on good manners, which goes for pets and humans. A well-mannered dog is a good reflection of its owner. A polite dog understands when to sit and when to keep off the furniture, how to wait patiently for food, and when it is inappropriate to jump up on visitors as they enter the house.

Nevertheless, teaching a dog can be challenging. The dog's owner and the dog must be consistent, patient, hardworking, and disciplined. Some dogs simply don't understand the rules or choose to disregard them when they feel like it, despite all the effort.

Then there's my dog, a low-riding moppet the shelter veterinarian claimed was a cross between the reputedly intelligent Corgi and Papillon breeds. My dog vehemently rejects any instruction that doesn't seem conversational. I can yell, "Stop!" and he ignores me, but if I say, "Hold up there, rug rat," he stops dead in his tracks. He may have taught me not to bark commands at him.

If you're not an expert dog trainer or are simply happy to let your dog be himself, giving commands might not come easy to you.

That doesn't mean you shouldn't attempt to train your dog to be well-mannered or, at the very least, to train him not to jump up on visitors.

Here are a few basic commands that every dog should be able to follow, along with instructions on how to teach them. You'll also need a leash, a collar, goodies, patience, and an authoritative alpha dog voice.

Teaching a Dog to Sit

Cesar Millan, a.k.a. The Dog Whisperer, claims that teaching a dog to sit entails a three-step procedure. Hold a goodie in front of your dog's nose to start. Next, raise your hand so his head follows the treat and his bottom descends. Say "Sit," reward him, and show him some love after he's settled. Continue until the dog understands the word.

How to Teach a Dog to Walk Nicely on a Leash

To start, choose whether you want your puppy to walk on your left or right side and be consistent. Then, "stand close to your puppy with the leash in a loose loop." and equip yourself with treats.

Treat "Fido" for being quiet and neatly seated or standing. Then, if or when the dog follows, take a step forward and reward him with a goodie. From there, continue rewarding your dog as you walk. If–or more likely when–the dog approaches you from the front, "turn the other way, call him to you, and reward him." Then carry on. Start praising your dog every other step at first, then every fourth or so, until they walk politely. Gradually start giving them fewer and fewer treats.

How to Stop Your Dog from Jumping on Visitors

The Animal Welfare League of Arlington claims that the key is to ignore inappropriate conduct. If your dog leaps on you when you get home, leave immediately and return later. "Wait for 30 to 60 seconds, then enter the room and enter quietly to welcome your dog. As soon as your dog jumps, walk away again and shut the door. Continue doing this until your dog stops jumping; stay with him and pet him as a treat. Treats can be kept on hand to incentivize the dog not to jump.

Teaching a Dog to Come

Put your dog's collar and leash on, get down on his level, and gently tug his leash while saying, "Come. Give him a reward and a pat on the head if he follows you.

Teaching a Dog to Stay

Reward your dog while having him sit. Then, reward him with another treat for maintaining the sitting posture. When your dog can remain still for a few seconds, gradually increase the distance by saying, "Stay," and moving backward. If the dog can stay, reward her with a treat before trying again from a farther distance. Continue building in steps, keeping it easy so your dog can succeed.

How to Teach a Dog to Leave Something Alone

If a puppy becomes overly inquisitive about something harmful, learning to "leave it" can help keep the puppy safe. Put a goodie in your hand to get things going. Show your dog the reward, then enclose it in your fist. Don't offer the treat to your dog if or when they attempt to get it. Say, "Leave it," and then wait for the dog to stop. Next, give the reward to your dog with the other hand.

Wait for your dog to move away from your initial fist before repeating the process. When it starts to walk away, say, "Leave it," and reward your dog while maintaining eye contact with your pet. Continue doing this until the dog learns that "Leave it" means she gets a treat.

How to Train Your Dog to Drop Something

"Drop it" can prevent your dog from eating anything it shouldn't, from chocolate to your favorite shoe, similar to the "Leave it" command. Like "Leave it," instruct your dog to "Drop it," and give your dog a treat when it does. Replace what you took from your mouth with something rewarding, such as a toy or a delectable treat.

Teaching a Dog to Lie Down

Keep the best-smelling item, such as cooked chicken or liver bits, in your closed hand. Afterward, raise your closed hand to your dog's face and move your hand to the ground when the dog sniffs it. The dog should descend while following the smell. The dog should be gently encouraged to place its entire body on the ground using your hand.

Once the dog is laying down, say "Down," then give the dog a reward and some cuddly scratches.

HOW TO BUILD TRUST WITH YOUR DOG

As caregivers, we consider having our canine friends' trust an honor. But what if your dog has encountered a situation that makes trusting people challenging? Is there anything you can do to give them the sense of security, self-assurance, and affection they need to trust you? Absolutely. You can tear down the barriers your dog has created with a little time and persistence.

Reasons Your Dog Can Have Trust Issues

Even though dogs are renowned for their unconditional affection, a variety of factors might affect whether they can trust people, including the person taking care of them. This can include surviving a traumatic experience or emotional scars from a history of abuse, lack of socialization as a puppy, and not being exposed to sights and noises like vehicle trips, children, and fireworks. Additionally, certain dogs' genetics can incline them to fear. A dog in a novel environment, such as one in which they have just been adopted, may take some time to warm up to and develop trust for new people, a new home, and a change in habit.

How Trust Impacts a Dog's Mental Health

Dogs who seem to trust you do so because they don't feel threatened or uneasy around you or in their surroundings. Making your dog feel secure is the key to developing trust. A trusted dog is confident that interacting with you will result in positive outcomes. Trusting dogs will actively seek out opportunities to socialize with those they trust. Your dog gains confidence as a result of this.

On the other side, a scared and worried dog won't seem to trust you and may avoid loving gestures like petting, be reluctant to play and partake in other enjoyable activities, and lack excitement when their human friend returns from work. Anxious and fearful dogs may run away from you or others and show little interest in communicating. If you try to push these dogs to play with you, they may snarl, bark, nip at you, or even try to bite you, so it's crucial to interpret your dog's behavior and avoid pressuring them into activities.

How to Build Trust with Your Dog

While it takes time and persistence to develop trust, there are many things you can do to make your dog feel more at ease and confident around you. Some advice might help you get started, depending on your dog's particular condition and how they express their trust concerns.

Recognize their body language. The body and face of a dog that is joyful and eager to greet you will be relaxed, and the dog will wag its tail vigorously back and forth while holding it high. A nervous or anxious dog may pace, avoid eye contact, hold their tail low or tucked under them, or exhibit any of the behaviors described below.

Observe further signs of worry and terror. These include carrying ears low or flat, crouching, moving slowly or standing still and stiff, raised hackles, trembling, a curling lip, growling, turning away, whining, lip licking, or yawning. If your dog exhibits extreme fear and anxiety, such as nipping, growling, adopting a frozen or stiff stance, biting, or running, set an appointment with your vet for evaluation.

Allow your dog to set the pace. Move at a pace that is comfortable for your dog. Progress will be slowed by rushing or pushing past their comfort zone.

Respect your dog's space. You might want to give your dog your undivided attention. However, timid and fearful dogs might not be quite ready for this. Move carefully, keep your eyes closed, and speak quietly as you give it some time.

Approach the dog at their level. Going close to dogs is crucial, as standing too tall might make them afraid and nervous. Either squat or sit on the floor to be at their eye level. Maintain a distance from the dog and ignore them until they approach you.

Allow your dog to approach you. When your dog approaches, respond in a cheerful, calm tone and give them a treat. Watch your dog as it consumes the treat. If they grab it from you roughly or drop the treat, they are likely feeling scared and nervous. Avoid petting the dog; speak to it quietly and give it a couple more treats. Then, let them have their space. You can continue if they take it from you gently and quickly consume it. Pet them by reaching your hand from underneath and, if they permit you, lightly caressing their chin or chest. Because a dog may feel threatened by a hand lifted over their head, it is vital to approach from below.

Use the "consent test" to check whether your dog is at ease with the interaction as you watch them while you touch them. As you pet them, count to three. Then, pause to observe if they lean in to receive more petting or let you know they appreciate the attention. If they withdraw, growl, adopt a stiff stance, or exhibit any of the symptoms above of fear and anxiety, allow them to stop the conversation with verbal praise. Give them their space. This promotes trust by showing your dog that you "listen" to their body language and respect their wishes about physical contact.

Be consistent. This encourages predictability, which encourages trust. Keep a regular schedule for feeding times, walk times, and playtimes. This helps your dog maintain the same expectations throughout the day, boosting their confidence and lowering the chances of any unexpected changes that occur evening to upset their sense of well-being. This uniformity should be observed by every family member, including using common verbal and nonverbal cues.

Provide a safe space. Dogs benefit from having a private area where they can safely hide from humans and other animals. Let your dog pick their safe place, and never invade your dog's safe spot or use it for punishment. Once they've found their safe place, you can make it a comfy space for them to retreat to by furnishing it with toys, a bed, or both.

Every time you or other family members walk by your dog, drop a tasty treat to help your dog form good associations with your presence. They don't need to take any action. They're only now beginning to equate people with food.

When she is calm and at ease, reinforce this behavior with praise and goodies.

Play again and again! The dog may forget their tension via play, which generates "feel-good" hormones, like dopamine. Playtime boosts the dog's confidence as long as it's having fun.

Simple shaping games are effective in developing trust. The goal is to work toward the desired behavior by rewarding even the smallest step in the desired behavior. For instance, if you want the dog to come to you, sit at the other end of the room. Say "yes!" firmly when the dog moves, whether by turning their head, extending a paw, shifting their weight, or doing anything else, and then tossing a treat to them. After doing this five times, toss the treat a few inches away from the dog but nearer to you. Repeat as your dog gets closer to you.

Start rewards-based training. Begin by asking your dog to sit, then praise them profusely while rewarding them with their preferred food item. Do this many times per day. Other commands like stay, shake, and down can be gradually added. Training sessions should be brief, positive, and enjoyable. Remember that the goal is to increase your dog's confidence rather than having a well-behaved dog.

Maintain a confident, calm demeanor and set an example. Dogs can sense both positive and negative emotions in the humans around them. If you encounter something your dog perceives as scary, keep your composure, talk softly, and take your dog away from the danger as soon as possible.

Professional support. You are not alone. If you require assistance, speak with a professional, preferably a licensed canine behavior consultant or a veterinarian with expertise in dog behavior. Your family veterinarian could know of someone in your neighborhood.

Helping a dog overcome their worries and anxieties is the key to developing their trust and confidence. Depending on the severity of your anxieties, this may require a lot of time and mental energy, especially if the dog has been abused, has had a traumatic experience, is prone to anxiety, or has been rehomed frequently. It might be difficult to lift a freshly adopted dog's spirits. Gaining your dog's trust will result in a better, more meaningful connection, making the work worthwhile.

CHAPTER 4: DEVELOPING IMPULSE CONTROL

It's not as important for you to manage your dog as it is for him to learn impulse control. Fortunately, it is possible to develop this crucial ability.

Once they have mastered a signal for "wait," most dogs can easily adapt their "wait" signal to other situations, including waiting to jump out of a vehicle, waiting to walk out of a door, and so on.

The behavior goes by different names, including inhibitive self-regulation, and emotional self-control, but in dog training, the phrase "impulse control" is usually employed. It indicates that dogs can exercise self-control and resist the urge to engage in undesirable conduct that would allow them to get a desired reinforcer.

Both puppies and kids do not naturally possess impulse control; it may be fostered and consciously taught. It is worthwhile to train your dog to manage his impulses since, as they do, we can unwind and enjoy their companionship without needing to supervise them constantly.

People generally don't think of a dog as having a self-control issue unless his urges cause him to display behaviors they don't like. Dogs are sometimes accused of lacking impulse control when they engage in behaviors such as helping themselves to food from the kitchen or living room counter (counter surfing), greeting visitors by jumping up on them, darting out the door when not asked, or stealing objects from their owners' hands. However, from the dog's point of view, a dog who exhibits these behaviors is only assisting himself in obtaining what he wants, whether it food, company from humans, freedom, a favorite toy, or any other item.

Fortunately, most dogs can learn to resist the urge to help themselves to these things by using delayed gratification or by using a few impulse-control strategies.

WAIT

I'll admit that training my dogs to "Wait" is one of my most practical behaviors–as well as my preferred exercise for impulse control. In contrast to a formal "Stay" cue, which implies "Stay in the exact position you're in and don't move until I tell you to," I use "Wait" to signify "Pause."

We use a food dish to teach the word "Wait." This allows you (depending on how frequently you feed your dog) one or two built-in sessions daily, so there are no excuses! The phrase "wait" may, therefore, be broadly applied to include waiting at doorways or in any other circumstance when you want your dog to be able to exercise restraint (e.g., from snatching the hotdog from the toddler's hand or refraining from lunging forward to meet the elderly person using a walker). How to teach it is as follows:

1. Sit your dog and tell her, "Wait!" Fill your dog's dish with high-value goodies and part of her normal food. If she is extremely driven by food, you can use her usual food as a reward, but the higher-value rewards will have a bigger impact.

Maintain the dish at shoulder height, tilted slightly to avoid placing it directly under her nose, and before she can (or does) move, mark her "pause" with a verbal marker, such as "Yes!" or "click!" using a clicker, and continue to say "Yes!" Next, offer her the treat you removed from the dish.

Say "Oops, sit!" and try again if she rises up before you click.

If she gets up after you've clicked and rewarded her, tell her to sit back down. Repeat, telling her "Wait" each time.

2. Tell her to "Wait," then lower the bowl a few inches while keeping it at shoulder height. If she's still seated, indicate (with a click or "Yes!") and rapidly bring the dish back up. After that, take out a treat and give it to her.

If she gets up as you're putting the dish down, try again, this time with the dish lowered just a little.

3. After many successful attempts at each new position, gradually lower the bowl by starting at shoulder height and urging her to

"Wait" between each one. If you say "Oops!" twice in a row, it means you're moving too quickly; go back up where she can succeed and drop the bowl more slowly.

4. place the bowl on the floor before rewarding your dog, click, and pick it back up. Say "Wait" a few times while repeating the phrase. (If she attempts to go for it, be prepared to raise the bowl fast.)

5. Next, click once you get the bowl to the floor, but keep it there as you reward the dog. Repeat the process severally, telling her "Wait" each time.

6. Finally, say, "Wait," place the dish on the ground, click, and reward her before saying, "Okay, you can have it!"

Dogs with superior innate self-control may "get it" after just one training session. Before you get the bowl on the floor, those more affected by their impulses might need to practice for a few days or longer. Work as long as it is feasible for you and your dog at each lunchtime practice session, and then place the bowl down on the ground while saying, "Okay, you can have it!"

With time and practice, you'll be able to instruct her to wait while you place the bowl on the floor, and she'll wait patiently for you to do so.

LEAVE IT

Shoes are required for this exercise! To teach the "Leave it" command, show your dog your tasty treat and allow her to watch you hide it inside your shoe. In a kind tone, say, "Leave it"; this is a hint, not a warning or a threat. Wait while she attempts to lick or claw the treat off.

I teach the command "Leave It" for the errant thing on the ground that my dog wants, but I don't want her to pick up. This is how:

1. Tell your dog she is not allowed to have a valuable "forbidden object" that you are holding in your hand. I use freeze-dried liver cubes as they are high-quality and durable. Allow her to sniff, lick, and even nibble at it, but keep it away from her.

2. As you raise the cube, say, "Leave It!" and instantly lay it on the ground beneath your foot to safeguard it. (Note: Put on sturdy footwear. Do not perform this while wearing your finest footwear, open sandals, or barefoot!

3. Allow your dog to explore the area around your foot by sniffing, licking, nibbling, and chewing. She could even paw at your shoe. Tip your toe forward if her tongue can reach the cube under your shoe so she can't lick it.

Just be patient—she'll give up eventually. When she stops sniffing, licking, or looking away from the treat, give her a yummy reward and mark (click "Yes!"). You may be able to remove your foot and still have her "leave it" as she becomes more adept at this behavior.

4. Wait. Don't give her the cue again; eventually, she will give up. Give her a pleasant treat and mark (click your clicker or use a vocal maker, such as the phrase "Yes!") the moment she stops sniffing, licking, etc., or looks away, even accidentally. Just wait a little longer; she'll likely return to the item under your foot immediately. Don't say the cue again. Mark and treat once more when she turns her head away.

5. If you can, mark and treat once more before she puts her nose back on your foot. You want to strengthen "Look-away, look-away, look-away, keep-looking-away" rather than "look at foot-look away, look at foot-look away."

6. After a few times, take up the cube, show it to her again, give her the "Leave It" command again, and then set it down beneath your foot.

7. If you see that her nose wanders away from the cube often, mark and praise her until she stops doing so. Even though the cube is plain to see and looks to be within reach, she gets rewarded for ignoring it. Hold on to your feet! If your dog attempts to steal food by diving for it, just cover it again with your toe. When her attention is diverted, mark or treat again.

8. Tap your toe near the item to grab your dog's attention if she's ignoring it, but be ready to quickly cover it up if that doesn't work. Keep in mind that you're aiming for a steady stream of "look-away" behavior, with no breaks in which she looks back at the cube.

9. At some point in training, your dog will have a "Aha!" moment when you can know he or she finally understands it. When she sees the exposed reward, she stops to consider it, and then she looks up at you, expecting a mark and a treat, and that is the moment you know you've successfully used Leave It. Celebrate!

10. Put the prohibited object on the floor without stepping on it (but be ready to!). Do this again and over again until you can leave it on the floor in front of her without her trying to steal it.

POLITE GREETING

Any dog's toolbox of impulse control skills should include this one. It demands that you lavishly encourage her for behavior like sitting while refusing to reinforce her for leaping up and preventing the rest of the world from doing the same. If she is free to wander, you can turn your back and walk away when she leaps up (or move into another room and shut the door). For more focused exercise, you can also use a leash or tether.

This little dog has a long history of being encouraged to leap up on kids (and biting and licking them), so it was crucial to use a tether to educate him not to do it again. Once stopped from reaching the kid, he learned to sit when he wanted to welcome a child.

1. Approach carefully and quietly When your dog is attached to something sturdy. Once she sits, mark (either with a clicker or a vocal marker like "Yes!") and give her a treat. If she jumps up, simply move back out of her reach. Note that we did not instruct you to say "Sit." Instead of waiting for a cue, we want her to execute that behavior on her initiative. If you need to help her in sitting, utilize body language (such as leaning back or bringing your hands to your chest; immediately fade the usage of this body language). Just refrain from using your standard Sit cue!

2. The energy of your approach should be progressively increased until you can welcome her with excitement. As she begins to regularly volunteer to sit when you approach (and you consistently reinforce these behaviors), she will continue to sit until you release her.

3. Now generalize the behavior to the rest of the world. Have someone else approach her as your dog is leashed. Tell them to approach cautiously and to retreat if she starts to spring up. Mark and treat her as though she has sat when they approach. Then,

they can say hello and pet her, but they should be reminded to retreat if she gets up.

If you choose, you might eventually ask the people approaching to reward her, but only if they understand that if she gets up, they must go.

MAT

Place the reward you use to reinforce any on-the-mat-behaviors on the mat. Your dog will learn from this that lying on the mat is rewarding! Every time she happens to lie down, give her the higher-value goodies; this will encourage her to do so more regularly.

The addition of the "place mat" is a genius development in the arsenal of force-free training. You can teach your dog to lie down and relax on a place mat, a portable rug, a bed, or a blanket. The training will be simpler if the mat is more comfy.

When your dog learns to park herself on her mat, you have a very helpful tool to aid with impulse control at home and in unfamiliar situations or with distractions that are certain to stimulate the senses. How to teach the behavior is as follows:

1. Hold the mat for your dog and show intense interest. Examine, discuss, and/or sniff the mat until your dog exhibits interest in what you are doing.

2. Lay the mat down on the ground. Have a selection of high- and medium-value goodies. Mark the mat and lay a medium-value reward for your dog to take when it looks at, sniffs, or displays any interest in it.

3. Put a medium-value reward on the mat each time you mark for any mat-related behavior (apart from grabbing and playing with it!).

4. She should be marked and rewarded for all on-the-mat behaviors (OTMBs), but if she gives a down, she receives a high-value treat. Other OTMBs still receive goodies of moderate value. Mark any OTMBs as you normally would, but periodically tell her to "Down" on the mat. Mark her when she does and reward her with a valuable goodie.

5. After cueing, marking, and treating a half-dozen random downs amidst her other actions, stop for a few seconds and see if she decides to give you a down when she isn't marked for other behaviors. If she does, mark her and give her several valuable goodies. If not, resume marking any OTMBs while incorporating cued downs. Deliver medium-value goodies for other behaviors and high-value treats for downs.

6. Carry on performing step 5 until your dog starts to offer down during your pauses. Your dog is figuring out that downs result in better treats. Even though other actions will still receive moderate rewards, she should eventually start exclusively providing downs on the mat.

7. Once you've invited your dog to follow you a few feet away from the mat, give her the cue to free herself. If she does, remain still and ignore her; do not give her any rewards or praise. Most dogs will come back to the mat to ask for more treats. (Go back to #5 if she doesn't.) If she does, you should start marking and rewarding her again, with larger treats for downs and smaller treats for everything else. You're helping her feel motivated to return to the mat. Ups are fantastic when they occur, but don't overlook the OTMBs. Distance yourself from the mat gradually.

8. When she regularly comes back and lays down on the mat when you leave, you may increase the time interval by a few seconds at a time. If she gets up before you can release her, pick up the mat, give her your whole attention for a time, and then put it back down.

9. When your dog consistently rests quietly on her mat, you can reinforce the behavior using the cue "Mat," "Place," or whatever you want to call it. As you become better at sending her from further and farther away, you can try sending her to her mat from anywhere in the house.

10. Add more distractions and make the conduct more widespread. Start with kindergarten-level distractions: clap your hands, hop once, twice, etc., working up to college level gradually when children are rushing through the home and spilling meals on the floor... Doorbell ringing, people walking in, and anything else that can make your dog's self-control difficult will eventually lead to PhD work. When she gets good at avoiding distractions at home, take it on the road and apply it to the rest of the world!

ON/OFF SWITCH

Your dog may occasionally become too excited by a stimuli. Since the presence of the leash is such an accurate indicator that "good stuff is about to happen," many dogs become quite excited when it does. Asking them to quiet down might backfire as you interact with them, making them more enthusiastic (and reinforcing their behavior!). I use "Oops!" as a "no reward marker.

When my dog jumps in excitement while I'm holding the leash, I say, "Oops!" and set the leash down on the table before going to sit down. I would exclaim, "Oops!" and put the toy behind my back or look away if I held one. If I were opening the door, I would say, "Oops!" and walk away.

Your dog has mastered impulse control when she can maintain her composure while you hold the toy, pick up the leash, or open the door. She can now manage her enthusiasm to make wonderful things happen.

I prefer using "Oops" instead of the "eh-eh" that some trainers use because it's difficult to pronounce "Oops" in an unpleasant tone of voice. The intention is not to be hostile or scary to the dog, only to provide information in a neutral or upbeat manner.

Your aim? Helping your dog practice self-control means you can have a relationship built on trust, respect, and love; it means you can relax knowing your dog will make the right choice even when faced with temptation; and it means you won't have to constantly play the role of behavior cop.

CHAPTER 5: BUILDING FRUSTRATION TOLERANCE

Why is it necessary to teach our pets how to deal with frustration?

The first and most important reason is that life is frustrating. Dogs will have to travel in cars. Unless you have food out all the time, they will have to wait for their meals. They will occasionally have to wait for activities like taking a stroll, getting in a car, or receiving a treat.

We often label pushy or impolite, persistent or impatient dogs as unable to handle even the slightest frustration. The duty is on us; we must realize that teaching young dogs this ability is necessary. In certain cases, the dog is caught accepting frustration instead of being taught. However, we also need to ensure we're setting our dogs for success as being unable to handle frustration may be an acquired skill.

When reward is withheld, frustration might develop. It frequently results from both operant extinction protocols and time-outs for dogs. This is a natural consequence of dogs not being taught patience in the face of delays between their requests and their rewards.

Understanding how to handle frustration is not usually something that just happens. Also, figuring out how to manage our emotions and behavior is not always easy.

You must begin by introducing errorless learning and fast reinforcement when teaching frustration. That is your baseline. Every activity in a program to increase the ability to tolerate frustration is a winner at the beginning. Starting from a point where nothing frustrates you is essential; otherwise, learning would be much more challenging. Whenever I work with dogs with mental issues or who want help, I always begin with substantial reinforcement on a continuous schedule for almost all behaviors.

#1 Scatter feeding

The use of scatter feeding is one of my favorite methods. You grab a bunch of treats; if your dog is very frustrated, use large, smelly treats. I'm referring to chunks of foul-smelling fish, slices of stinky meat, and Stilton lumps and Parmesan shavings. At first, scatter heavily and densely.

How do you level up? Alter only one variable at a time. Better disperse the food. Make it harder to find than it already is. Use fewer and smaller odorous bits. Use less food.

Why does scatter feeding help in teaching frustrated dogs coping mechanisms? Because the time between appetitive behaviors (such as searching) and consummatory behaviors (such as eating) is getting longer and longer. Dogs learn to persevere and develop resilience via scatterfeeding. Frustrated dogs are also frequently worried, and I find that this develops abilities that aid in their relaxation. I'm unsure how or why it happens, but I've always likened scatterfeeding to dog yoga. The odors linger on the ground, which helps prevent the frustration of things coming to an end. As food availability decreases, you also create endurance and a tolerance for frustration in the exercise.

#2 Free work

This also holds true for scheduled free work periods. If you still haven't found any free work, get help from an expert. It was designed by Sarah Fisher and is often used to evaluate the posture and general health of dogs. I utilize it completely differently, depending on the purpose; however, if I'm using it to build frustration tolerance, I use it in a very precise manner. The free work was meant to help people notice the animals in their life, but Sarah would probably be happy to see it being used to enhance the skill sets of humans and dogs alike.

You start with an easy set. The food is in easy reach. There are no challenging frozen Kongs or Noses that only spit out one treat every two hours. Nothing is difficult to access. Surfaces are low and non-challenging. I use a variety of things all the time, such an old pile of clothes, a silicon snake, a Kong, a firm mat, and a stuffed marrow bone. I'll also add things like the bone marrow that can entice the dog to linger.

I've seen that irate dogs will not even tolerate food that requires many bites or chewing sessions. Even that could be challenging. I've seen dogs give up on Kongs that were frozen, packed too tightly, or stuffed with paté.

After that, we advance, just as you do with scatter feeding. We occasionally include a foraging exercise or a more frustrating food toy in our planned and systematic routine. I put in fewer morsels of food, and they have to struggle for the food. I also include non-food items like boxes of things with different fragrances and scent libraries. I tuck nibbles into the pockets of the worn-out clothing and cover goodies with a mat. Everything becomes increasingly difficult with time.

How can you train a dog that cannot stand being frustrated for ten minutes? You begin with one second. Then two.

#3 Plan the Goldilocks increments

Whatever you do, ensure your strategy is "just right," like Goldilocks. Too straightforward, the dog won't learn to handle frustration any more than it already does; too difficult, the dog will become more frustrated.

Most individuals are awful at this. They take enormous steps. They start with one second if their dog can't wait 10 minutes for what they want. Next, they switch to a full minute. Never perform at a level that is less than 5% of your previous one and never go over 10% of your next one. If your overly dependent dog can't be separated from you for more than five minutes without wailing, start with five seconds and build up from there. Even six seconds is a 20 percent increase. As a result, you must slice and dice your criteria very thinly.

#4 Use Tug games creatively

I love tug of war. If you are unsure, I realize it's not for every dog. Tug is a safe and cooperative play, so I greatly like it. Dogs and humans don't work together very often when they play. The dog doesn't know about your relationship as you are just a machine that launches balls. While they are cooperative, I use wrestling and sparring very sparingly when dealing with irate dogs as they are not for every dog. Furthermore, games like Chase Me and Hide and Seek might be a lot of fun. Because cooperative games make it clear that we won't always succeed, they help us learn how to handle frustration. The game ends if one person becomes demanding or pushy. Additionally, it establishes boundaries and encourages dogs to take turns. You have distinct cues for engaging and disengaging.

I would advise against playing tug with a really irritated, yappy, or noisy dog, but it is something to think about as you work on building your dog's tolerance for not getting the toy. If you want to teach the dog accuracy, you may also begin with very long tug ropes.

You can start by utilizing a variety of long rope toys (up to one or two meters) to play brief, quick games. The dog becomes too eager, so you let go of your end, grab another, and go again. They are starting to realize that if they let you know how frustrated they are, they can win the toy, but the game will no longer be fun.

#5 Teach the Counting Game

Make sure you are proficient at reducing arousal levels before using free work settings or engaging in games. An aroused dog is more prone to display signs of frustration. But if depriving the dog of anything makes him miserable, how do you achieve that? I often scatter-feed games and interrupt them at will.

I love the Counting Game for so many reasons, not the least of which is that it's a great diversion in an emergency and a great option for dogs that struggle to part with resources. Its special power is in situations when you don't want to aggravate your young, loud, and irascible dog who is destroying things and finding it hard to play without becoming agitated.

Therefore, even though the game must end, dogs that "win" the tug toy are more likely to get overstimulated and less able to handle the game ending. I take a step back and begin handing out rewards. I may smear some paté, peanut butter, or cream cheese on top if I need to dial it down. Chewing or licking is preferable.

DESENSITIZATION AND COUNTERCONDITIONING

Two training techniques, desensitization, and counterconditioning, may aid in your dog's recovery from reactivity and adverse feelings toward certain people, animals, or other stimuli. If your dogs show signs of fear or anxiety, develop a consistent strategy founded on tested techniques to retrain your dog's mental processes and behaviors.

What Is Desensitization?

The desensitization training method is one of the most frequently suggested techniques to help your dog overcome anxieties. Desensitization is a method of behavior modification that gradually exposes your dog to their phobias at low levels while gradually raising the intensity over time to educate them not to respond adversely.

Desensitization promotes your dog's understanding that their fear is unfounded. Desensitization training will make a stimulus your dog was previously sensitive to look inconsequential or just like any other thing your dog isn't fearful of. Desensitization training is often paired with counterconditioning training.

What Is Counterconditioning?

Counterconditioning is a training method frequently used in conjunction with desensitization training. If your dog reacts negatively to stimuli, counterconditioning may change your dog's response from something undesirable to something desired or from a negative reaction to a positive one.

Imagine, for instance, that your dog would rush at the window, bark, snarl, and scratch up the windowsill each time a person walked by your house. It is necessary to transform these negative and undesirable behaviors into good emotions and desired actions. Counterconditioning training can help your dog reverse this behavior by assisting your dog in associating the individual strolling by with a pleasant experience. In this behavior modification, incentives include food, attention, verbal praise, unique toys, and other types of positive reinforcement.

How to Modify Your Dog's Behavior Using Desensitization and Counterconditioning

Depending on the exact behavior, circumstance, and pet, some dogs may take longer to relearn what they have been conditioned into, but if you are consistent and patient, you can make good improvements.

Determine Your Dog's Triggers

Is it a person, an item, a sound, or a smell? Once you identify it—which may need some observing skills—you may start the training by exposing your dog to its trigger in a way that won't make them feel terrified, angry, apprehensive, etc.

To pinpoint the real cause, it is essential to recognize the subtle indicators of fear and anxiety in dogs. The dog will occasionally start acting subtly before becoming more aggressive and appears to be reacting to something that isn't the trigger. For instance, if a dog first displays nervousness at the mailman but then starts to bark and act aggressively against a housemate or other person. We must recognize the initial signs of dread and anxiety and retrain ourselves to respond to that trigger.

Practice Positive Reinforcement Around the Trigger

If an item is the source of unpleasant thoughts or behavior in your dog, you should first keep it far away from your dog. Ensure that your dog can view the object without being upset by it. Reward your dog when she knows her triggers and doesn't react negatively. This incentive might be a special treat, your dog's favorite toy, or verbal and physical praise.

If you cannot store the object somewhere semi-permanently, leave it here for a while, often a few days, or expose it to your dog every day for a few hours. Slowly bring the object closer to your dog over time, rewarding them each time they look at it without acting undesired. You can move the object back a little to slow down the procedure if your dog reacts badly as you bring it closer.

Don't Scold Your Dog

Instead of scolding your dog when they respond inappropriately, reward them when they don't react so they can learn to identify the trigger with a positive outcome. Your dog could eventually start to disregard the object. Your dog will eventually be in close proximity to the object, but they will already be desensitized or aware that there is nothing to be scared of. Due to the continuous counterconditioning training, the dog will also link the object with pleasant things like rewards, toys, praise, and caressing.

Start Small

You can combine these two training methods when your dog reacts unpleasantly to odors, sounds, or even people. If a weak scent or soft sound is the trigger, start with that and work up to a stronger or louder fragrance. If the trigger is a person, start with someone far away and gradually bring them closer, just as you would with an item.

Be Patient

Regardless of the trigger, it's critical to remember that these training sessions occur on your dog's schedule, not yours. Go through your training schedule with your veterinarian. They could have suggestions for supplements that might alleviate anxiety and promote learning. Helping a pet feel less anxious about something should hasten the training process and enhance results.

Desensitization and counterconditioning won't work if you try to hasten things. Avoid overstimulating, frightening, or forcing your dog into anything, as doing so might worsen matters. Instead, you want your dog to gradually relax and learn to associate the trigger with something positive. Only by being patient and attentive to your dog's emotions will you be able to do this.

CHAPTER 6: STRENGTHENING THE HUMAN-CANINE BOND

Even though animals cannot speak, the bond between dogs and people is quite deep.

There are truly special ties that develop between people and animals. But how does it happen?

The basis for the dog-human relationship

We are all aware of several factors contributing to the special bond dogs and pet owners create. In this respect, a team of researchers under the direction of Michael Tomasello from the Max Planck Institute in Leipzig, Germany, have produced academic publications that seek to explain how dogs raised in households can decipher their owner's gestures to locate hidden food. Researchers discovered that people and dogs share an attachment relationship that enables them to assist one another, like the link between a mother and her child. Further study has revealed that dogs and people communicate in remarkably comparable ways. This is the reason a strong bond is formed.

Dogs vocalize their feelings in a way that is quite similar to how people do; in fact, dogs appear to react to weeping and the many emotional states that people exhibit via speech.

Dogs' genes have evolved significantly through time to the point where they have begun to behave like humans. Pets living in our society produce more oxytocin, sometimes known as the "love hormone," than people do. As people and dogs have spent more time together, the production of this substance has grown, and as a result, so have the social bonds between the two species. As a result, the bond between dogs and humans has a long history and was primarily made possible by their adaptation to other species' communities via evolution.

How to improve your relationship with your pet

Over time, a pet parent's relationship with their pet deepens and grows. However, a few easy steps can be taken to improve this affinity and strengthen bonds.

1. Educate the animal properly

Education is important for both people and animals. By helping your pet become more self-aware, basic training may greatly deepen your relationship with him or her. Additionally, it's crucial to begin educating them from their earliest months.

2. Quality time

Spending time with your pet is crucial if you want to deepen your relationship with him. Giving him or her attention, whether it be on a stroll or a trip, is incredibly important to help them feel loved and valued.

3. Play together with your pet

Playing with your pet is releasing after a long day of exploring. It's unlikely that you always have the stamina to leap or run after him, but your pet doesn't need to. The most crucial thing is playing and cuddling him to show him you care.

4. Communicate effectively

A good pet parent should never be wary of getting to know their furry friend, even if it means researching the traits that make a particular dog breed unique. Dogs are unique; therefore, it's necessary to make an effort to comprehend how they behave. A great method to improve communication with your dog is to ask a dog trainer for guidance.

Benefits of the dog-human relationship

The relationship between a dog and a pet parent has several advantages.

First, pet owners are more compassionate and kind toward all animals.

On the other hand, animals are extremely sensitive, can tell when a person is upset or angry, and can alert you to their presence. The gratification is undoubtedly mutual.

Nothing comes close to the bond between a pet parent and their animal companion. It is a sincere and pure relationship that will not be easily broken.

EXPLORING THE EMOTIONAL CONNECTION BETWEEN A DOG AND THE OWNER

Those who have dogs tend to think their canines are good at reading their moods. This is not something made up in their heads. Dogs can distinguish between their owners' fear, enthusiasm, or rage thanks to behavioral and physiological clues from humans, according to studies, and they can also "catch" these emotions from their human counterparts.

Dogs typically look to humans for cues on how to interact with other animals and people, just as human infants learn social norms through watching their parents. Dogs are more likely to feel comfortable and secure in their surroundings when their owners project an air of calm and assurance.

" The bond between people and dogs is founded on shared feelings of love and loyalty," claims Clive Wynne, a psychology professor. Dogs are incredibly sociable, making them susceptible to catching our warmth and delight. However, the inverse is also true, meaning that the tension and worry of the owner can also affect the dog.

The psychological, physiological, and behavioral underpinnings of this "interspecies emotional contagion," as psychologists refer, are present. Recent research has shown that a range of physiological factors, such as the release of specific hormones (like oxytocin), alterations in human body odor, the firing of particular neurons in dogs and their owners, and others, can affect how emotions are transmitted.

Recent research indicates that the length of a relationship has an impact on how much a person and their dog are able to sense one other's feelings. For the time being, that phenomena is especially noteworthy, given the amount of time individuals spend with their dog pals.

A primitive form of empathy

Dog and their owners may have a range of emotional bonds with their pets, from understanding and identifying one other's moods to actually feeling the same emotions together.

Studies show that dogs are able to recognize our yawns, respond emotionally to our voice tones, and, similar to humans, experience an increase in cortisol when they hear a newborn cry. Oxytocin, also referred to as the "cuddle hormone" or the "love hormone," is released when humans and their dogs interact or even simply stare into each other's eyes, according to research. But the hormone's effects are more nuanced than that; under certain conditions, it fosters generosity and trust, while under others, it fosters jealousy.

Larry Young, professor of psychiatry, says that bonding is a feedback loop that occurs both between humans and dogs. Social touch, such as petting, or eye contact, may produce oxytocin. "Dogs must be able to perceive their owner's emotions to experience emotional contagion; this requires attentiveness, which oxytocin enhances. It directs the brain to pay attention to social cues."

Additionally, dogs show "affective empathy"–a term used to describe the ability to understand the feelings of another person–for people who have a special place in their hearts. Genuinely sharing such emotions is referred to be emotional contagion, a primitive kind of affective empathy. For example, in a 2020 study published in the Canadian Journal of Experimental Psychology, researchers examined the reactions of dogs when their owner or a houseguest feigned to laugh or weep. The dog showed more physical affection and made more eye contact with the person who seemed to be crying. Associate professor of psychology at Ripon College in Ripon, Wisconsin and co-author of the study Julia Meyers-Manor claims that the dogs' stress responses were heightened when the stranger wept.

According to Meyers-Manor, contagious emotions are a part of all forms of empathy. In some respects, feeling what another animal feels is simpler intellectually than detecting another [creature's] emotion.

When people converse, they automatically mimic the body language, facial expressions, posture of their conversation partner, which frequently results in people sharing another person's emotions. Because of the gradual muscle movements involved in this phenomenon, mirror neurons–brain cells that react to an action, like smiling, as well as when it is observed–fire, triggering the actual feeling in the brain and giving you the impression that you are actually experiencing it. It turns out that dogs engage in rapid mimicry when they play or interact with one another, and it may also be triggered when canines interact with humans.

Meyers-Manor notes that when dogs and people are furious, their facial muscles are frequently tensed, their teeth clenched, and their bodies stiffen. As a result, when confronted with an angry dog or while feeling agitated, you may unintentionally imitate each other's body language or facial expressions and experience the same emotions. Meyers-Manor said, "We evolved together to identify each other's [emotional] signals in ways that differ from other species because of our close connection with dogs."

It was long thought by experts that emotional contagion emerged during the domestication process as a means of survival for dogs; after all, if dogs could read and feel what their owners were experiencing, they would get better care. That's a more evolved way of thinking in recent times. A research that was published in Scientific Reports suggests that the oxytocin release that takes place during interaction between dogs and their owners is caused by their connection and shared experiences. Furthermore, a 2019 research that was published in the journal Frontiers in Psychology found that the longer a person and their dog partner spend the same space together, the more emotional contagion occurs.

Body odor and Facial expressions

Sensory elements can also influence the emotional contagiousness of people and their canine friends. According to experts, dogs are remarkably adept at reading human body language and facial expressions. According to some studies, cCnines perceive human facial emotions similarly to humans, while others have indicated that canines pay more attention to the body than facial clues when displaying emotion. According to a 2018 study published in the journal Learning & Behavior, dogs' gaze and heart rates vary in response to human faces expressing the six primary emotions of anger, happiness, sorrow, surprise, fear, and disgust.

According to Monique Udell, an animal behaviorist, dogs often imitate their humans' natural movements, so it's not unexpected that they coordinate their emotions.

“Since dogs frequently mimic their owners' natural movements, it is not unexpected that they coordinate their behavior. Dogs and people also frequently express the same emotions. Dogs are highly attentive to us, and some of this observation is based on our gaze and body language, as well as on the noises we make and the odors we give off."

On the auditory front, studies have shown that dogs react differently than other vocalizations or non-human noises to sounds that suggest sorrow, such as sobbing, or happiness, such as laughing. Dogs are more likely to look at or approach their owner or the source of the sound when they hear specific human noises.

According to Wynne, "dogs are extremely sensitive to body odor–it's how they can identify epilepsy [in people] and possibly diabetes [in people]." In an experiment described in a 2018 edition of Animal Cognition, Labrador and Golden Retriever puppies were exposed to samples of three human body scents that stood in for fear, happiness, and a neutral emotion. After inducing these feelings in the male volunteers, the researchers collected odor samples from their armpits. Then, in an area where the dogs could wander about unrestrictedly while being among either their owners or others, these scents were aerosolized by a unique dispenser: The dogs' stress levels and heart rates were higher when they were exposed to the smell of fear than they were when "happy" odors were present; furthermore, the dogs' curiosity in the strangers was higher when happy odors were present.

Professor Emeritus of ecology and evolutionary biology at the University of Colorado, Boulder Marc Bekoff states that dogs frequently use combined signals, which incorporate information from multiple senses, such as hearing, sight, smell, and possibly touch if the dog is anxious.

All canines are not born equal, either in terms of mentality, physicality, or socialization. As each dog is unique, Bekoff suggests getting to know them. People generally ask me, "You must be fluent in dogs." Bekoff counsels dog owners to observe their dogs' facial expressions, barking, body language, and other vocalizations to see what messages they are conveying to them.

A bidirectional effect?

In general, dogs' emotional spectrum is probably less than most people's. In my opinion, dogs' emotions aren't particularly nuanced, says Wynne. They "experience cold primal emotions like anxiety and fear and warm primal emotions like excitement and happiness." Beyond that, there are still a lot of unanswered questions, and one of the difficulties in conducting this sort of research is that dogs are unable to express their emotions precisely at any given time.

While some experts think it's extremely likely, research haven't looked into the possibility of humans picking up emotions from their canines. According to Wynne, "I certainly feel that my dog's happiness can lift my mood." Bekoff concurs, saying, "I absolutely believe we pick up on their emotions. It might be easier to sense their worry and fear at times. However, if a dog approaches you with its tail waving and ears pointed forward rather than backward, that dog is likely to be happy.

Whether they're dog owners or not, people are quite proficient at reading the facial expressions of dogs to determine both positive and negative emotions. This is in part because both humans and dogs exhibit similar changes in facial expression when expressing particular emotional states, according to study.

Leash reactivity is one example that demonstrates stress and tension may spread in both directions: While you're walking your dog on a leash, if your dog lunges, barks, growls at other dogs, cars, or people you can feel stressed out or embarrassed, which can make you stiffen up and aggravate your dog's anxiety. According to Udell, this "can be a trigger for the dog doing it again," which can start a vicious cycle.

However, sharing each other's emotional highs and lows tends to be generally positive since it fosters stronger connections and has survival significance. “If you think about our forefathers, having a dog that could warn you to anything so you could respond swiftly was a matter of life or death. The two-way roadway on the alarm side benefits both [species] in turn,” Wynne says.

The human-canine bond is enhanced by sharing a place to live, a family, and activities. Sharing our emotions with one another "helps us to comprehend each other better, and it promotes the bond that develops and how it's maintained over time," according to Bekoff. "Emotional connection between dogs and people is like social glue." It holds us together firmly, often for the rest of our lives.

CONCLUSION

A reactive dog is never easy to own. It might be difficult to balance everyone's needs for safety and pleasant relaxation and help your dog work on reactivity.

One of the most prevalent problems many dog owners deal with is dog reactivity. Dogs can respond negatively to stimuli, including humans, other dogs, loud noises, and objects. Understanding the causes of your dog's reactivity and employing efficient training methods will help lessen it and enhance your dog's behavior in general.

Dog walks with your reactive dog can be mentally and physically difficult and might test traditional views of proper canine behavior. Acknowledging your thoughts about your dog's conduct and embracing your dog's discomfort is important to help you feel motivated to carry out a training program. You and your dog will enjoy calmer, happier walks for years to come if you address your dog's emotions and teach them more positive alternatives.

If you are facing this difficulty, realize that you are doing great, no matter what phase of your journey.

Don't forget to scan the QR Code to get all bonus content!

Made in the USA
Las Vegas, NV
15 November 2023